Kicking Those Habits

Written by Stephen Sallis Wilburn

The C. R. Gibson Company
Norwalk, Connecticut 06856

Copyright © MCMLXXXV by
The C.R. Gibson Company
Norwalk, Connecticut 06856
Printed in the United States of America
All rights reserved
ISBN 0-8378-5403-2

INTRODUCTION

Let's face it—no one is very expert at kicking habits. We all know people who seem so self-disciplined that we imagine they have control over every aspect of their lives. And sometimes these people can appear so priggish, so self-righteous that we take some comfort in our own bad habits. At least we're **human**, we tell ourselves, not machines. Thus we appease our consciences.

But people are "human." People we know who always **seem** to be doing the right thing (the ones with a balanced checkbook, neatly pressed clothes, never a run in their pantyhose or hole in their sock) are also troubled by bad habits. Like an allergy in spring and fall, habits keep coming back in one form or another. It seems there are always things we do and wish we didn't. Even as vigorous and committed a man as St. Paul says, **"the evil which I would not, that I do."** (Rom. 7:19).

We do the same things every day, maybe several times a day. Maybe most of our habits do not hamper our lives. They do not prevent us from doing our jobs, cooking dinner or shoveling the snow. But in our best moments, we want to be rid of them. Usually there are at least

INTRODUCTION

two very good reasons for doing so:

1. Those habits are noticeable and unattractive: fingernails bitten to the quick, caffeine or nicotine-stained teeth, that slight bulge around the waist.
2. Something else is running our lives and it shouldn't be. We might as well call it by name: it is sin. Now, nobody is going to hell because of an unwelcome habit. But sin is slavery. The glorious secret of service to Jesus is **freedom**. That's what bad habits keep us from, and that's what Christ cares supremely about.

Our habits define the sort of people we are. Are we in the habit of caring about the little needs of others? Then we probably care about the big needs. Are we quick to forgive the spilled milk? Then we know how to turn the other cheek. Are we free enough to drive right past the pastry shop every day? Then we are truly free to enjoy the odd donut with the children on a Saturday morning. **Freedom** is the issue, not perfection.

Don't believe those people who suggest that if you only had will power you could break that bad habit in a breeze. It's not that easy, but it can be done and you will gain far more than you lose. You will gain the chance to be

INTRODUCTION

what you want to be, the kind of person you should be.

The seven steps that follow are the preliminaries. They are practice, like the scales every piano student practices to play Chopin someday. Once you've gone through them all, there are still habits to face. But perhaps then they can be faced. By clearing away other impediments, a habit may not seem so stubborn. Take these steps at your own speed and in your own way. And remember, God is with you. It is the Holy Spirit who finally deserves the credit. Let us simply clear all those hurdles we have placed in the way of knowing Godly freedom.

STEP ONE

Decide for Freedom

Then said Jesus to these Jews which
believed on him, "If ye continue in my word,
then are ye my disciples indeed;
and ye shall know the truth,
and the truth shall make you free."
They answered him, "We be Abraham's
seed and were never in bondage to any man:
how sayest thou, ye shall be made free?"

Jesus answered them, "Verily, verily,
I say unto you, whosoever committeth sin
is the servant of sin...
If the Son therefore shall make you free,
ye shall be free indeed."
Jn. 8:31-34, 36

STEP ONE

Perhaps it seems too harsh to call unwelcome habits sins. It will help us, however, if we look beyond the more dramatic examples of sin. Sin, in the singular, suggests not so much a deed, an act, as it does a condition. The condition of sin is a type of slavery. We are not free from it. Everyone knows that it is easier to commit a sin the second time around. It is addictive in a sense. So, bad habits are an example of our bondage. It is something we have trouble escaping. By definition, it is hard to be free from those habits.

Complicating this condition is our all-too-human tendency to accept that condition. It is not so much that we are hopeless, more that we just do not stop to think that we might be free.

The Israelites were slaves; they were in bondage in Egypt. The Egyptians were their masters. They were forced to live in Goshen. They were forced to labor long and hard for the Pharaoh's tombs. They had no choice but to labor without rest—making bricks. In short, they were not free; they were slaves.

No doubt, most of the Israelites had come to accept this as an unchangeable condition of life. (Think of people living today under cruel and oppressive regimes; they have no choices.

STEP ONE

The vast majority of them know of no other way of life than simply accepting their lot.) The children of Israel knew of no way out. They could only try to make the best of a bad situation, difficult as it was most of the time.

Then God sent the Israelites a man named Moses. And ever since that time, more than three thousand years ago, Moses has been known as "the great deliverer"—the man that God used to bring the Israelites to freedom.

God even prefaces the Ten Commandments (Exodus 20) with that reminder: **"I am the Lord thy God, which have brought thee out of bondage."** That is the kind of God He is and He chose Moses: the Bringer of Freedom. God wishes you to be free.

Freedom is available to you; you only have to **decide** to take it. So, that is our very first (and maybe the most important) step in kicking our habits. Today, it is time to take that step. Here are a few ideas to help you make that decision:

- We all have tricks to help us remember things, like a string around the finger. Find something to symbolize your decision to be free.
- Hang a large wall calendar in the room where you spend the most time, the kitchen,

STEP ONE

for instance. On the day you decide to seek freedom, put your own private mark on that day on the calendar. Mark the anniversary of that day each month. Simply decide. That much isn't hard. But it is necessary and important. (Don't tell anybody, yet, what you are planning to do. This will be your own private resolution.)

Dear Lord, help me to desire the things You desire for me. I want to be free from these things that hold me back. I count only on Your help. In the name of Your Son, my Deliverer.
Amen

STEP TWO

Sort Out Your Habits

For ye have not received the spirit of bondage again to fear; but ye have received the Spirit of adoption.
Rom. 8:15

Some habits are worse than others. Most of us have several undesirable habits. So the next thing we need to do is to sort out this part of our lives. Perhaps you bite your fingernails, indulge in cookies or potato chips much too often, rub your chin when you're nervous, stay up too late at night, sleep too late the next morning and you're often late to work. Where do you start?

STEP TWO

This is one instance when the easy way out may be a very good place to start. You need to **feel** what it is like to break a habit. You may recognize "patterns" of behavior in your life, certain regularities that are so trivial they really don't deserve to be called "habits." Well, that is a very good place to start.

I admit it. I play solitaire! For years it was my habit to start the game over again if the first card I turned up was a king of any suit. There was a reason for this at the outset, I'm sure. I probably thought that if I turned up a king to begin with, the game was a loss from the start. When I thought about it, this was not what I really believed (I was probably cheating, anyway!). But I was in the **habit** of doing it. Realizing that I was at the mercy of a pretty silly attitude, I stopped being quite so predictable. At first, I flinched, but pretty soon I forgot what all the fuss was about. So it was a king. So what? I had broken a very silly and inconsequential habit! And I felt more in control of myself. The point is: start out easy to get the feel of breaking habits.

This is where a bit of self-analysis is needed. One of the best ways to do self-analysis is to make lists. (I am a great believer in making lists.) To take a first step start making these lists:

STEP TWO

- Write down all your habits, good, bad or indifferent. (This is for your eyes only.) Carry a card or a sheet of paper around with you for a day or two to jot down more habits as you think of them. Try to find at least twenty habits. I bet you won't have any trouble finding that many.

- Find an hour when you can be alone and undisturbed. Then, divide that list into three categories: **1) Now, 2) Later, 3) Never.** Place your habits into each category. "Now" might be those you think you can begin working on. "Later" might be those that are really dependencies, too tough to handle now, or those that are going to take a little practice to deal with. "Never" could well be those that you wouldn't part with for love or money! Take the "Now" list and divide it into two columns. Call one column "A Piece of Cake" and list there those trivial habits that you think are the easiest to break. Call the other column "Oh, Boy" and list there those habits that are going to take a bit more in the way of effort and concentration.

- Take the next step. Pick the easiest one of all, the one that matters the least, and start to learn what it feels like to kick a habit. Once you've been free of the habit for a week, re-

STEP TWO

ward yourself with a splurge. (Read a book you've been wanting to read for a long time, listen to a soothing record.) Enjoy your freedom!

Dear heavenly Father, since I am Your child, today I count on Your help to do what I could not do if I were left to myself. Through Your Son, Jesus Christ, I pray.

Amen

STEP THREE

Pick a Card, Any Card

Stand fast therefore in the liberty wherewith Christ hath made us free, and be not entangled again with the yoke of bondage.
Gal. 5:1

There are people who make self-improvement a bleak and dreary process. They improve because they're mad at themselves. They may end up with plenty of broken habits, but they are really worse off than before they started. Whatever joy was in their lives is gone. And they also succeed in depressing most of the people around them. They have "improved" for the wrong reasons. Life is not meant to be lived through gritted teeth!

STEP THREE

The end product of freedom is supposed to be joy. If it doesn't produce joy, then it isn't freedom. It's just another form of slavery. Joy is a calm assurance, a smiling serenity. Joy can take a joke. If you approach the prospect of kicking a bad habit in the same frame of mind as taking a cold shower, something's wrong. Your imagination has fooled you into thinking that **doing without is misery**. It isn't. It can be delightful. It can be, if you believe it, **fun**.

In the previous step you chose a habit that was easy to change, to stop. You did this for practice, to feel what it was like to make a change. Now pause to consider a real, live, unwanted habit. Pick one. From the list you made, sort out one bad habit from among the others. Choose it from the "Now" list. We're not ready to kick it just yet. But we have got to concentrate on one and one only.

There are no criteria by which to choose the one, except that it comes from the "Now" list. You could put slips in a hat, cover your eyes and pick one. The point is, it doesn't matter which one you choose. In fact, it **shouldn't** matter. You do not want to pick one because it's too hard, too easy, too important, or for any other reason. If you chose that way, then you'd probably be trying to kick this habit for the wrong

STEP THREE

reason. The reason is wrong because reason does not work. If it did work, you would have kicked that habit long ago! Now then:

- Assign each habit now on your list a number. Tell your best friend to choose a number between one and ten (or five, or thirty) and take that number to concentrate on.

- Write the number and the habit down on a 3" × 5" card. Put that card in your wallet or your purse, or put it in one of your pockets; read it several times a day; do not fold it or the card will be too easy to overlook. You'll know it's there all day long, you won't forget about it, and only you will know that you have claimed it.

The idea here is to take one step at a time, one habit at a time. When you first made your lists, you may have felt overwhelmed by all the things that needed attention. Now, address them one at a time. You can't deal with them all at once. Remember, we're not in a hurry.

Gracious Father, never let my efforts prevent Your Spirit from controlling my life; help me do what I need to so that habits will not control me either. In Jesus' name.

                                              Amen

STEP FOUR

Think About It

O Daniel, servant of the living God, is thy God, whom thou servest continually, able to deliver thee from the lions?
Dan. 6:20

Sometimes mental tasks are the most difficult to face. They are difficult not because our minds are weak (although we often use that excuse) but because our minds are so changeable.

But eventually thoughts and feelings will coalesce. And then our thinking doesn't seem so nebulous or indistinct. Suddenly it is concrete. And our minds seem clearer.

Daniel, in the middle of hungry lions, had a

STEP FOUR

mental task to perform. What could he do? Fight the lions? Protect himself? So unequal were the odds that there was nothing at all he could do. Still, his mind had work to do. Daniel needed to stifle his utter terror and concentrate his trust on God. How did he do it? What did he do? We are not told, but I would like to make a guess or two. I imagine Daniel first **accepted** his situation. Then with no escape, he could turn his mind to other matters. Two resolutions of his situation were apparent: One: the lions would tear him limb from limb. Two: they would not. **What if they did?** Daniel thought. **I am safe in the hands of the Lord, whether dead or alive. And if they did not? Then I am still safe in the hands of the Lord.**

As you face a troubling habit, think about yourself as safe in the hands of the Lord. Whether you kick that habit or not. You need to be very clear about that habit—to know what it is and what it is not. Are you mixing up more than one bad habit? Then take one at a time. Do you bite your fingernails as a reflex action, not really thinking about it? Then find a way to be aware when you bite your fingernails. Concentrate on it; think about it; don't let it get away.

But most important of all, imagine what it

STEP FOUR

would be like to stop, to do without that habit. Imagine long, smooth fingernails, firm and healthy. Use your imagination to transport yourself to a beach or to the stage of an important theater or to an opulent country home. Now use that same imagination to carry yourself in your mind's eye away from that habit. Imagine your life without that third cup of coffee before ten o'clock in the morning. Imagine driving to work without a donut to munch on. Make it a game; force yourself to concentrate on this problem and this problem only.

There is only one exercise for this stage:

- **Talk to yourself.** Out loud. Not, of course, when anyone is within earshot! Discuss the problem with yourself. Ask yourself why you haven't done anything about this habit before now. Give yourself a good answer. Be honest with yourself. Describe to yourself (out loud) in colorful detail what it will be like without that bad habit hanging like an albatross (which is a pretty big bird) around your neck.

O Lord, this habit of mine is like an angry lion, and I have nowhere else to go. Shut its mouth. Take away its

STEP FOUR

power over me. Clear my mind. Help me to place my life into Your strong hands. For Jesus' sake.

Amen

STEP FIVE

Behind the Curtain

As free, and not using your liberty for a cloak of maliciousness, but as the servants of God.
I Peter 2:16

I remember the first time I moved away from my parents' home. In distance it was a major move, from Mississippi to Chicago. More important was the psychological move away from the spoken (and implied) rules of home. I suddenly had more raw, absolute freedom than I had ever had before. And that freedom proved to be fertile soil where all sorts of habits flourished. It may be a universal experience. Sudden and total freedom is so exhilarating we tend

STEP FIVE

to revel in it. Then we discover that we are enslaved to something else. Once we were rolled firmly out of bed on school mornings; now we are free to sleep late whenever we choose. If we let ourselves indulge in that glorious, extra hour in the morning, sooner or later it becomes harder and harder to get to classes or work on time. A bad habit has taken root.

Habits seem simple. This I do; this I wish I didn't do; this I will not do. "This" doesn't seem to be the issue. "Do" is the problem. But there is in reality more to it than that.

That habit you want to kick is a sort of curtain. Something lies behind it! And that "something" may be the **why** of the habit. Your next step is to peer behind that curtain and come up with a reason or two. This need not be self-therapy or heavy introspection. In one sense, this is an extension of the last step; it is another way to think clearly about this habit.

Say you munch a bag of potato chips every night before going to bed. There are more empty potato chip bags in the trash than paper napkins. Worst of all, you can now "pinch an inch" around your middle with ease. Why? Something as simple and definable as that potato–chip habit has you by the throat and

STEP FIVE

won't let go. It's no good bemoaning your lack of self-discipline; there are probably dozens of chores you do daily and freely and joyfully. Why munch potato chips of all things?

There might be all sorts of reasons (childhood deprivation?) behind that curtain, but they don't really concern us right now. The issue is freedom; it can turn on us. The very thing we want (liberty) may have caused the problem in the first place. We first acquired this habit because there was no one around to stop us. Besides, we're grown up now; we don't want people telling us what to do. We're free. Right?

Wrong. Instead of obeying parents or the police or the law, we are now obeying something else: convenience, indulgence, expediency, comfort. There is an itch somewhere deep within our gray cells, and a long time ago we came up with what we thought was a scratch for that itch. But the itch is still there; only now we gratify it with a bag of potato chips in our hands. A good scratch never made an itch go away.

St. Peter says with the same breath, be free, be a servant. A contradiction? No. Because serving God is the only service that sets us free from everything else. That's precisely what God has in mind. Obedience to anything else (and they

STEP FIVE

are things, not a Person) requires further obedience. Indulgence is a cruel master because indulgence can never be satisfied.

Back to lists:

- Try to remember when you first began this particular habit. At the top of your list, write down **why it.** This may not be easy. And there may be more than one reason. But write them down, even if they seem trivial. They're not.

- Now, make a list saying why you continued this habit. There are reasons for habits. One good reason is a mild form of fear: I'm afraid of being bored, of not having anything good to taste, of doing without, of the void. Don't worry if this list-making causes some shame. Shame is a very private thing, it won't kill you, it's good for you, and it will go away.

- Once you have made the list of "whys," look at it in private and say, "This is the way I am…now." This is an important exercise of self-acceptance.

There are no "simple" souls. We are all complicated individuals with layer upon layer of meaning to our lives. You are a worthwhile,

STEP FIVE

valuable person. The aim of this whole business is to free you to be what God intends you to be.

To You, dear Lord my Master, I offer all that I am. Take me as I am and love me. Give me Your grace in Your way in Your own time and that will be sufficient for me. In Jesus' name.
Amen

STEP SIX

Some Things Take Time

I am the Lord thy God, which have brought thee out of the land of Egypt, out of the house of bondage.
Ex. 20:2

The story of Moses and Pharaoh, of slavery in Egypt and escape through the Red Sea is one that always needs to be remembered. It is the original story that tells everyone what sort of God there is and how He operates. This story defines God, defines His people, defines the way He acts. It is a sort of real-life parable. We are in slavery in Egypt. God wants badly for us to be free. He will do something about it. Over and over again in the Old Testament when

STEP SIX

God has something to say to us, He begins by saying who He is: **"I am the Lord thy God, which have brought thee out of the land of Egypt, out of the house of bondage."** Ex. 20:2.

We can read the story of the Exodus in an hour or so. But we can lose sight, then, of how much time it took. The sons and daughters of Jacob had been slaves for a very long time. None of them knew any other kind of life. While they were miserable with the sort of life they led, it cannot be said that they were impatient; they probably felt that any release from their lot was so far out of the question that it was not worth thinking about. Then Moses arrived. Their first reaction to him could well have been derision ("You're kidding, right?"), then ridicule ("Freedom? What an absurd thought!"), then came the first glimmer of hope ("Maybe?"). In due time, for a few, there came real belief. But with that belief came another problem: growing and gnawing impatience. Each time Pharaoh "hardened his heart," hopes were dashed and impatience grew worse. Which is worse, to be without hope or to have hope crushed?

It shouldn't be hard to apply the Exodus story to our struggle with habits. As long as we live

STEP SIX

with them, we are living in bondage. God intends for things to be different. He will provide a way. We need to follow Him through our own personal Red Sea.

The emphasis here is patience. It takes time to bring ourselves to the point where we want to do something about our habits. Kicking them, too, will take time. Earlier you used your imagination to create a situation where you were rid of one habit. It takes several weeks to be really at the point where you no longer even think about it. So make **time** a part of your mental picture. Those several weeks will be a testing period. You might grow impatient with yourself. You might even fail. None of that matters. It's perfectly normal and natural. It doesn't mean that you have failed permanently. It is merely part of the process.

You must be patient with yourself while coming to the point of actually beginning to kick that habit. Only **you** will know when the time is right. Furthermore, only **you** will know when patience turns into procrastination. What you want most of all is a new style of life, a life where you always have the freedom to deal calmly with habits that have accumulated over the years.

STEP SIX

- Remember your wall calendar from the first exercise? You made your own personal mark on it the day you decided to do something about your bad habits. How long has it been? Make another mark exactly four weeks from the first one. On that day you will re-evaluate how far you've come and how far you have yet to go.

- Make another mark six weeks from the first one. That will be the day you start to kick that habit. You will know that day is coming and it will help you focus your mind on the task at hand.

Gracious God, help me to see my life as You see it. Grant me the patience I need, but keep me from putting this business off longer than necessary. For the sake of Your Son, Jesus Christ.
Amen

STEP SEVEN

For the Long Haul

O give thanks unto the Lord:
for he is good; because his
mercy endureth for ever.

Let them now that fear the Lord say,
that his mercy endureth for ever.

I called upon the Lord in distress:
the Lord answered me, and set me
in a large place.
Psms. 118:1, 4, 5

We can now speak of the "habit of living free." But we have used the word "habit" in a different sense. Here we mean it to be "practice" or "character" or "the usual way of doing

STEP SEVEN

things." Instead of being prey to habits we have no control over, we are approaching a mental level where we are aware of the things we do and now we are ready to eliminate those that are unhelpful or even harmful.

All the previous exercises have been meant to prepare us to begin kicking a habit. This last one is the same, but it is the last one. Then comes the momentous step, the first day you forego that donut or that wad of chewing gum or biting your fingernails.

There are a number of helpful things you can do to help yourself:

- If biting your nails is a problem, you need to be aware each time you start to bite. Rub some cinnamon (or another fragrant herb) on your fingers—not enough to be noticed, but enough so that you'll taste it. You'll remember.

- Find substitutes for your habit. Anything will do, however unrelated to your habit. Instead of a cup of coffee as soon as you wake up, brush your teeth and make that the first thing you do when you wake up. Instead of a bag of potato chips at night, find something detailed to do with your fingers while watching television. If television is a problem (con-

STEP SEVEN

stantly watching TV can be nothing more than a habit) then at some point during the day make a list of other things you can do in the evening: Start a program of reading books aloud to someone else, do needlework, or clean a closet.

- My son has become very good at helping me not pick at my fingernails. He says nothing, all he does is reach over and simply touch my hand. I'm more grateful to him than I can say. It works. Sometimes it helps a great deal to bring someone else in on what we're trying to do—someone we love and trust. The last thing we need is any sort of guilt over failing. We're probably going to fail at first. So be sure that anyone you let in on the secret **will let you fail**, then help you start all over again. That's a friend indeed.

O loving Father in heaven, since You made me, You know me. Help me come to be the full person You made me to be. Give me Your Grace to kick this one habit, and then extend Your love for me further so that I will always lead the kind of life You want for me. In Jesus' name.

Amen

CONCLUSION

The reward of following these steps is meant to be satisfaction and freedom. It is not happiness—not the sort of happiness that (falsely) promises giddiness. We are looking for satisfaction that lasts a good deal longer. Soon we will know with a calm, deep certainty that whenever we notice something in our lives that needs changing, we can change it. We will know it because we have practiced it. We are not in the clutches of anything else, and we have come to a sort of Godly control over our lives.

In the Bible, the great promise is for Eternal Life. This is not meant to suggest only an endless succession of years, but a promise for a certain quality of life. It is life lived under the Lordship of the Eternal. This is what we are meant to grow toward. It is not arrived at by gritting your teeth or exerting your iron will. It is rather a life filled with the Eternal One.

Those bad habits we have collected should not be the main packing material in our lives. These exercises are intended to clean up our lives the way we clean up a new house before moving into it. It is one good way to "prepare the way of the Lord."

CONCLUSION

"It's easy to quit smoking," said one wag. "I've done it hundreds of times!" It's easy the first time you consciously decide to quit any bad habit. The trick is to stop the habit, and that is a daily, even hourly thing. Be patient with yourself. Use your wall calendar and take one day at a time, one week at a time, one month at a time. Finally, never fail to remind yourself just how far you've come, and take great satisfaction in that very important fact. With God's help, you have become free!

Designed and illustrated by Miggs Burroughs

Typeset in Eras book, medium, demi, and bold